HANDS-ON SCIENCE

FOOD AND THE KITCHEN

Step-by-Step Science Activity Projects
from the Smithsonian Institution

Gareth Stevens Publishing
MILWAUKEE

For a free catalog describing Gareth Stevens' list of high-quality books,
call 1-800-341-3569 (USA) or 1-800-461-9120 (Canada).

ISBN 0-8368-0955-6

Produced and published by

Gareth Stevens Publishing
1555 North RiverCenter Drive, Suite 201
Milwaukee, Wisconsin 53212, USA

This edition © 1993 by the Smithsonian Institution. First published by
the Smithsonian Institution, and Galison Books, a division of GMG Publishing,
as a series of Science Activity Calendars.

Series editor: Patricia Lantier-Sampon
Book designer: Sabine Beaupré
Editorial assistants: Jamie Daniel and Diane Laska

Printed in the United States of America

1 2 3 4 5 6 7 8 9 98 97 96 95 94 93

CONTENTS

Weights and Measures Abbreviation Key

U.S. Units

in = inch	oz = ounce	
ft = foot	qt = quart	
tsp = teaspoon	gal = gallon	
T = tablespoon	lb = pound	
C = cup	°F = °Fahrenheit	

Metric Units

cm = centimeter	kg = kilogram
m = meter	km = kilometer
ml = milliliter	°C = °Centigrade
l = liter	
g = gram	

INTRODUCTION

By the 21st century, our society will demand that all its citizens possess basic competencies in the fundamentals of science and technology. As science becomes the dominant subject of the workplace, it is important to equip children with an understanding and appreciation of science early in their lives.

Learning can, and does, occur in many places and many situations. Learning occurs in school, at home, and on the trip between home and school. This book provides suggestions for interactive science activities that can be done in a variety of settings, using inexpensive and readily available materials. The experiments, activities, crafts, and games included in this book allow you, whether teacher or parent, to learn science along with the children.

SOME SUGGESTIONS FOR TEACHERS

The activities in this book should be used as supplements to your normal classroom science curricula. Since they were originally developed for use in out-of-school situations, they may require some minor modifications to permit a larger number of children to participate. Nonetheless, you will find that these activities lend themselves to a fun-filled science lesson for all participants.

SOME SUGGESTIONS FOR PARENTS

One of the most important jobs you have as a parent is the education of your children. Every day is filled with opportunities for you to actively participate in your child's learning. Through the **Hands-On Science** projects, you can explore the natural world together and make connections between classroom lessons and real-life situations.

FOR BOTH TEACHERS AND PARENTS

The best things you can bring to each activity are your experience, your interest, and, most importantly, your enthusiasm. These materials were designed to be both educational and enjoyable. They offer opportunities for discovery, creative thinking, and fun.

HOW TO USE THIS BOOK

There are ten activities in this book. Since every classroom and family is different, not all activities will be equally suitable. Browse through the book and find the ones that seem to make sense for your class or family. There is no prescribed order to these activities, nor any necessity to do all of them.

At the beginning of each activity is a list of all the materials you will need to do the project. Try to assemble all of these items before you begin. The procedures have been laid out in an easy-to-follow, step-by-step guide. If you follow these directions, you should have no difficulty doing the activity. Once you complete the basic activity, there are variations that you can try, now or later. At the end of each activity is an "Afterwords" section to provide additional information.

SAY CHEESE

SAY CHEESE

In only an hour and a half, you can make fresh cheese, but you must start the project a day in advance. For best results, read through the recipe before you begin.

YOU WILL NEED

½ Gallon very fresh whole milk
¼ Cup cultured buttermilk
Salt
Large Pyrex or other heat-resistant bowl
Large pot (big enough to hold the large bowl)
Cheesecloth
Colander
Knife, spoon
Plastic wrap
Small bowl

If you accidentally leave a carton of milk out on the kitchen counter all day, what happens to it? Is it spoiled? Sour? Unsafe to drink? Bacteria in the milk are multiplying and dividing as fast as they can. But don't think all bacteria are harmful. The bacteria that make milk sour are *not* harmful. Actually, they are essential to making yogurt, sour cream, and many kinds of cheese.

6

Here's a recipe for making soft, fresh cheese from milk that's been left standing too long. The first time you try it you might get a very soft cheese like cream cheese. Or you might get firmer chunks, or "curds," which means that you've made cottage cheese. Either way, you'll be surprised how easy it is to make a delicious and nutritious food.

BEFORE YOU BEGIN

To go on with Steps 2, 3, and 4, you'll need to be around at just the right moment, when the milk has "clabbered." The amount of time this takes will depend on two things: how much buttermilk you use and the temperature of the "warm spot" where the milk is standing (have someone check this with a room thermometer). The chart at right will help you plan ahead by showing *approximately* how many hours it will be until the milk clabbers and the curds are ready to be cut. (But check the milk early.)

Temperature	Clabbering Time
60 °F	44 hours
70 °F	23 hours
80 °F	17 hours
90 °F	13 hours

1 Let ½ gallon of fresh milk stand in its carton for several hours, until it reaches room temperature. Pour it into a clean, large Pyrex bowl and set the bowl in a warm place. Add ¼ cup buttermilk to the bowl and stir well. Cover the bowl with plastic wrap. Don't bump, move, or jiggle the bowl after this. Let it stand undisturbed overnight.

2 Within the next 24 hours, the milk will become soft, like a custard. This is called "clabbering." When the milk has clabbered, you will see the watery-looking whey collecting on top of the curd and at the sides of the bowl. Now it's time to cut the curd into cubes. Use a knife to make cuts, about ½ inch apart, through and across the curd, to form squares. As you cut through the curd, the "custard" should split and separate into distinct ½-inch-square cubes with clean, sharp edges. If that doesn't happen, your clabbered milk is not quite ready to be cut. Wait a little while and then test it again.

3 After you've cut the curd, let it sit for 20 minutes. Meanwhile, fill a very large pot half full with hot tap water and set it on the stove. Then gently carry the bowl of curds and whey to the stove and set it inside the big pot of water. Now you must heat the curds *very slowly* to make them coagulate (clot) more and to release more of the whey. Use a low gas flame or low setting on an electric stove and bring the temperature of the curds and whey up to about 100°F. If you don't have a thermometer, ask an adult to stick a clean finger in the whey. At 100°F it will feel quite warm, but not hot enough to make the person jerk the finger out. Be sure to heat the curds *slowly:* It should take *at least 30 minutes* to bring them up to 100°F.

4 Remove the bowl from the big pot. Pour the hot water out so you can use this pot to drain the cheese. Set a colander inside the big pot, and line the colander with two layers of cheesecloth. When the curds and whey have cooled slightly, about five minutes, pour them — gently — into the colander to drain. Occasionally pick up the four corners of the cheesecloth and shake the cheese, so that more whey can drain off. If you are making cottage cheese, you can twist the top of the cheesecloth "bag" and squeeze.

5 Remove the cheese from the cheesecloth and put it into a small bowl. Add salt to taste — between ½ and 1 teaspoon should be right. Refrigerate your cheese immediately, and then enjoy it!

Caution: Although the bacteria in the milk are harmless, other types of bacteria may get into your cheese before you are finished making it. *If at any time your cheese looks spoiled or smells bad, don't eat it.*

HINTS FOR SUCCESS

■ If your milk doesn't clabber within 24 hours, it probably never will (unless you have left it standing at 60 °F; see the Clabbering Times chart). You may have to start over if that happens. Use more buttermilk next time, and / or place the bowl of milk in a warmer spot.
■ Don't break the curds or stir them while you are cooking the cheese. The smaller the curds are, the more whey they lose. If they lose too much whey, your cheese will be too dry.

AFTERWORDS

There are more than 400 kinds of cheese made throughout the world. But, believe it or not, all cheeses — from Swiss cheese to blue cheese to Camembert — start out as milk and undergo the same basic procedures you experimented with in Say Cheese. Some cheeses are cooked a little longer than others. Some curds are stirred and some are not. Some are pressed only lightly, and others are put under 100 pounds of pressure for several days. And some cheeses are eaten right away, while others are left to cure for two months or more in deep, cool cellars or caves. All of these changes in method have an enormous effect on the final taste and texture of the cheese. But perhaps the most important factor is the ripening or curing process; that's when the bacteria can *really* go to work. Bacteria are the heart and soul of cheese. Without them, milk wouldn't get past the liquid stage.

The bacteria present in milk, fresh from the cow, are called *lactobacilli*. When they feed on *lactose* (milk sugar), they don't get fatter — they just divide in half and multiply.

During their feast, lactobacilli give off a waste product called *lactic acid,* which first sours milk and then causes it to coagulate. (Yogurt and buttermilk are made this way.) Later, when the coagulated milk has been made into cheese, the bacteria continue to break down the protein in the cheese. This improves the texture and taste of the cheese.

However, most of the bacteria present in milk are destroyed during the pasteurization process. But 1% of them do remain, and those can be encouraged to multiply by adding some similar bacteria from a "starter" culture. When you made cheese, you added buttermilk as a starter culture, and you really didn't know what kinds of bacteria you would get. Cheese manufacturers, however, want to choose their bacteria very carefully. They have many different species, each one suited to making a particular kind of cheese.

As cheeses ripen and cure, they are often allowed to form their own rind, which seals the cheese and prevents other, unwanted bacteria from penetrating it. But some-

times — as in the case of blue cheeses such as Roquefort, Stilton, and Gorgonzola — mold is either encouraged or even added to the cheese on purpose. For instance, moldy bread crumbs are mixed into the curds to make Roquefort. On the other hand, Gorgonzola develops its blue-green veins all by itself when the cheese is pierced through to allow air to enter.

Of course, when it comes to cheese, the age-old question is: "How do they put the holes in Swiss cheese?" For the answer, just look for cheese's best friend, bacteria, again. Certain types, or strains, of bacteria produce gas, which gets trapped in little pockets in the cheese. As the gas expands, the cheese is pushed out of the way and holes form In fact, you can tell how old a piece of Swiss cheese is by looking at the size of the holes! If the holes are small, as in Baby Swiss cheese, you'll know that it was cured for a shorter period of time; it will also have a milder flavor. For a stronger flavor and aroma, choose a Swiss cheese with larger holes.

ANTS IN YOUR PLANTS

ANTS IN YOUR PLANTS

Each Ants in Your Plants experiment takes about 10 minutes to set up. The amount of time you spend observing the ants is up to you.

YOU WILL NEED

1 Spoonful of tuna
    or meat scraps
1 Spoonful of honey
    or maple syrup
1 Piece of fruit
    or other picnic food
Jar lid, bowl of water, stick

What would the ants eat if you invited them to your picnic? Would they go for the salami sandwich first or head for the watermelon? Invite the ants in your plants (or lawn or park) to a picnic just for them. You may be surprised by their special ant antics.

BEFORE YOU START:
Can an Ant
Make You Say Uncle?

Ants belong to the family Formicidae of the order Hymenoptera. This may not seem important until you realize that bees and wasps belong to the same order. Some ants have stings and some can spray poison from the end of the abdomen. Most ants have strong jaws and will bite to defend themselves and their nests.

The bite of one tiny ant can hurt a little. The bites of many ants can hurt a lot. That is why you must be very careful when dealing with ants.

■ When ant hill hunting, always wear protective clothing, such as long pants tucked into high boots. Heavy socks will help.

■ Avoid disturbing ant colonies. If you step in the wrong place, your legs will be covered with ants before you know it.

■ Don't try to pick ants up with your fingers. Use a stick or other utensil to keep a healthy distance between you and the ants.

EXPERIMENT No. 1:
HILL HUNT

1 Go on a hill hunt on your lawn or in your park to find an ant hill. An ant hill looks like a small pile of dirt with a hole right in the middle of it. Sometimes when you spot an ant walking through the grass, you can follow it back to its hill. If you can't find an ant hill, find a bare spot on the ground to do your ant hunting.

2 Put a small spoonful of tuna or meat scraps about one foot away from the hill or the center of the bare spot on the ground. A spoonful of cat food will work, too.

3 Pour a small spoonful of honey or syrup on a leaf. Lay the leaf about one foot away from the ant hill or bare spot. Make sure it is also at least one foot away from the tuna or meat.

4 Set out fruit and any other kinds of picnic food you think the ants in your plants might enjoy. Put each kind of food one foot away from the ant hill or bare spot and one foot away from any other kind of food.

5 Watch carefully. Which kind of food do the ants find first? With each food placed one foot from the ant hill, the ants will choose their favorite foods, not just the ones closest to them. Some ants like meaty food like tuna and insects. Other ants would rather eat sweet foods like honey and plant juices.

Do the ants eat the food on the spot or do they carry it back to the hill? Do they work alone or do they help each other? As you observe the ants, you may notice that when an ant finds food, it runs back to the hill to "tell" the others. As it runs, it leaves a trail that other ants in the hill can smell. The ants find the food by smelling their way along the trail. You can use these "smell trails" to make more observations about ants.

6 Find a place where several ants are going back and forth on the same smell trail. Lay a stick across the smell trail and watch what happens.

7 Carefully scoop up a few ants. A paper plate may be useful for this purpose. Gently put the ants on the inside of a jar lid. Float the lid in a bowl of water. The ants can't escape because they can't swim. You can also keep them from wandering by coating the edge of the jar with petroleum jelly or grease.

8 Place a piece of tuna or meat in the jar lid with the ants. Watch to see if they eat it. Check if there is more than one kind of ant on the lid. Do the different ants fight over the food? Which type wins?

After making your ant observations, go back and look at the pieces of food and sweets you placed around the ant hill. Are they still there?

VARIATIONS

■ Some ants come out in the open to eat only at night. Perform the Hill Hunt experiment at night. Use a flashlight to check for new kinds of ants feasting on your food bait.

■ Can your mother smell as well as an ant? How about the other members of your family? Make a smell trail on your lawn or in your park and let them try. Put several spoonfuls of extract—peppermint, coconut or almond—in a spray bottle or mister. Fill the bottle with water. Make a trail by spraying the extract every six feet in a line. See if your family can sniff its way from beginning to end.

HOW TO BE AN ANT FARMER

You can buy an ant farm kit in a pet store or through a catalog, but it's much more fun to make your own. Get a large, clean glass jar and fill it with soil. Set it in a pan of water to keep strays from wandering off the farm. Lay a piece of cardboard with a small breathing hole in it on top of the jar. Coat the rim of the cardboard with petroleum jelly or grease.

Place the ants from your lawn or park in the jar with care. Start out with at least two dozen. Try to add a queen

THE ANT FARM

HOLE
CARDBOARD
GREASE
JAR OF SOIL
WATER IN PAN

ant to your farm so you can watch the whole life cycle. The farm won't last long without a queen. You may find it worthwhile to buy ant eggs to populate your farm. Feed the ants dead insects and corn syrup. Give them a wet sponge or cotton ball to suck on for water. Soon the ants will dig tunnels and rooms as they go to and fro along their smell trails.

AFTERWORDS

Ants are just about everywhere. You can prove this fact whenever you go on a picnic. Just find a nice picnic spot without an ant in sight, spread out your blanket, unpack your picnic basket, and suddenly it's ant city. Where do the ants come from? They probably were living in the ground right under your picnic basket. Many kinds of ants live underground in ant cities called colonies. Each colony is ruled by at least one extra large queen ant. A queen ant can live as long as fifteen years. Her job is to lay eggs to produce more ants for the colony.

Ant colonies can contain thousands of ants. Most of these ants are worker ants. The workers build and maintain nests and hunt for food for the queen, for the young ants, and sometimes for soldier ants that defend the nest from invaders. Worker ants carry this extra food in their second stomachs. Their first stomachs are used for their own food.

The way some ants collect food is fascinating and almost human. One type of ant keeps tiny insects called aphids like farmers keep cows. Aphids suck the sweet juice or honeydew from plants. The ants like to eat honeydew. To get the honeydew from the aphids, the ants "milk" them by gently rubbing them with their feelers. In the winter, the ants bring the aphids into the nest.

Other kinds of ant farmers cut pieces out of leaves. They chew the pieces until they are soft, then spread them out underground. Soon, a fungus grows on the chewed leaves. The other ants eat the fungus.

Some worker ants in the desert use their second stomachs to store honeydew. These workers are fed any extra honeydew. They get so fat, they can hardly move. They just hang in the nest like little honeypots. Other ants take honeydew from the honeypot ants.

While worker ants feed the colony, soldier ants protect it. One type of tree-living ant guards the nest by grouping their heads together like a door. They open the door to let colony members in and out, and shut the door to keep other ants out.

Tailor ants in Asia, Africa, and Australia sew leaves together to make nests. The ants living in bullhorn acacia trees in Mexico live in the trees' thorns. The tree makes nectar for the ants to eat. The ants protect the tree by getting rid of insects and animals that try to eat it. The tree couldn't live without ants. Tree-living ants are just one variety of ants that don't live underground. Ants live in nests in dead wood, in living plant tissue, or in papery nests attached to twigs or rocks. Ants also may invade buildings or ships.

The driver ants of Africa have no permanent nests at all. They are almost always on the move. When millions of these ants are on the march, they eat everything from insects, birds, and small animals to large animals such as elephants. They have even been known to eat people who could not get away. When driver ants are on the march, people don't worry about ants spoiling their picnics. They worry about becoming the main course at an ant picnic.

12

PIZZA GEOGRAPHY

PIZZA GEOGRAPHY

Pizza Geography will take about 90 minutes to complete and eat using ready-made pizza dough. Add about 2½ hours to make the crust from scratch.

YOU WILL NEED FOR ONE PIZZA

8 Ounces tomato or
    pizza sauce
½ Pound grated mozzarella
    cheese
Sliced vegetables
    (onions, peppers, etc.)
1 Cookie sheet (11" × 15")
Spices (oregano, garlic,
    basil, etc.)
Sliced cooked sausage
    or pepperoni
Any other topping
    you would like to try
Oil, oven
Rolling pin or drinking glass
Atlas or other book of maps
Camera (optional)
Ready-made dough
    or ingredients at right.

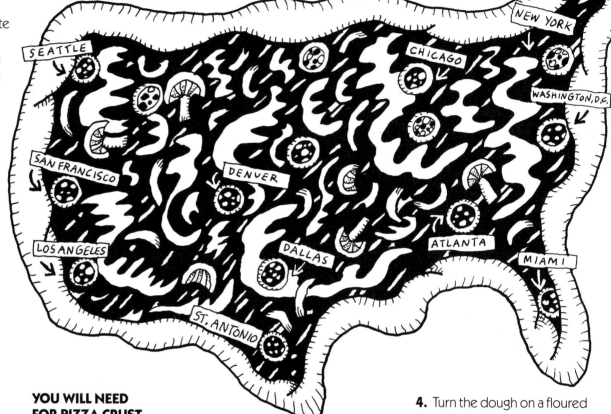

YOU WILL NEED FOR PIZZA CRUST

¼-Ounce package
    dry yeast
1⅓ Cups warm water
2 Tablespoons oil,
    1 teaspoon salt
1 Tablespoon honey or sugar
4 Cups flour
1 Freezer container
Mixing bowl, clean dish towel

1. In a mixing bowl, dissolve the yeast in warm water.
2. Add oil, salt, and honey *or* sugar. Mix well and let stand for five minutes.
3. Add the flour one cup at a time. Mix between additions. Add flour until dough is elastic, but sticky.

4. Turn the dough on a floured board or counter and knead for a few minutes. Kneading means folding and pressing the dough. Check a cookbook for more details on kneading, if needed.
5. Oil a mixing bowl and flop the dough into it so the dough gets coated with oil. Cover the bowl with a towel.

Let the dough rise in a warm place for 1 to 1½ hours or until it is double in size.

Yield: Two 11" × 15" pizza crusts. (You can freeze one-half of the dough after it rises. Place it in an airtight freezer container. When you want to use it, just defrost the dough, punch it down, spread it on an oiled cookie sheet, and add toppings.)

A map can be more than just numbers and lines, and a pizza can be more than just topping and crust. Put a map and pizza together for a fun dinner that you can design yourself.

1 Make the pizza dough. If you are in a hurry, buy a ready-made pizza dough or crust mix. While the crust dough is rising, look through an atlas (a book of maps). Decide what type of map you are going to make (weather, population, major rivers, etc.).

2 Preheat the oven to 425 °F. Coat a cookie sheet with oil. Plop the dough onto the cookie sheet. Wet your hands with oil or water so the dough won't stick to them as much.

3 Squeeze and press the dough onto the cookie sheet. Use a floured rolling pin or glass to help you flatten it out.

4 Use an atlas to help you form the dough into a map of the U.S.A. or another country. Make a ridge of dough along the edge to keep sauce and toppings from dripping. Spread tomato sauce over the dough.
■ Add toppings to mark features: mountain ranges and rivers; your state, state capital, and towns where friends and relatives live; favorite vacation spots; historic landmarks;

major industries or crops or other important or special spots.

5 Photograph or draw your pizza map. This will be your "before-baking" picture. Once the map goes in the oven, the cheese will melt and spread. Your map will look different after it has been baked.

6 Bake the pizza map for 20 to 30 minutes. The baking time will depend upon your oven and the thickness of your crust. Keep checking. The pizza is

done when the cheese melts and the crust is brown.
■ While the pizza bakes, play Geography. What is the capital of Delaware? Where is Glacier National Park? Think up questions to ask each other. The answers can be found in the atlas.

7 When the pizza is done, take it out of the oven and let it cool. Photograph or draw your "after-baking" picture. Now eat the pizza.

AFTERWORDS

If your idea of geography is memorizing the names of the Great Lakes, then you probably think geography is boring. In fact, geography is a fascinating subject, because it covers the whole world. The word *geography* even means "writing about and describing the Earth." Geography includes both natural features of the Earth, such as rivers and mountains, and man-made features, such as bridges and cities. It helps describe the Earth from ancient times into the future. Geography is concerned with all of the forces that change the Earth, from hurricanes that wipe away coastlines to wars that wipe away national boundaries. But geography does not stop on Earth. Geography has also conquered space with maps of our solar system and beyond.

Geography covers such a wide area that no one can handle all that needs to be done. Here are some of the special jobs that geographers do:

■ Biogeographers study the living things on Earth and map their locations. Their maps show jungles and grasslands and rain forests and prairies, and what animals live in each environment. Biogeographers must know life sciences and earth sciences as well as geography.

■ Demographers are population specialists. They study how and why human populations change. For example, they would study why people seem to be leaving cities to live in small towns. Their maps would show these changes.

■ Medical geographers put contagious diseases on the map. They help decide who can travel where, and what shots may be needed before going.

■ Economic geographers look at how people earn money and how that affects where they live. They study people whose farm animals graze on grass; they also study automobile workers whose jobs depend upon industry.

A geographer's job is to describe changes on the Earth's surface, but it is even more than that. He or she must often attempt to explain why the changes occur and to predict what will happen in the future.

Geography is a lot more than a game about state capitals.

1/4 oz = 7 g	1 1/3 C = .32 l	2 T = 30 ml
8 oz = 227 g	4 C = .96 l	1 tsp = 5 ml
1/2 lb = .23 kg	1 T = 15 ml	425° F = 218° C
11 in x 15 in = 27.9 cm x 38 cm		

GINGER ALE

GINGER ALE

1 T = 15 ml	1 C = .24 l
3 T = 45 ml	2 1/2 C = .6 l
4 qt = 3.8 l	

Ginger ale takes about an hour and one-half to prepare. It must be bottled after six hours. Ginger ale will taste best if you wait two days before drinking.

YOU WILL NEED

Pot filled with 4 quarts water
3 Tablespoons ginger
½ Lime
2½ Cups sugar
3 Tablespoons cream of tartar
1 Tablespoon baker's yeast
Cheesecloth or coffee filter
Funnel, mixing spoon, stove
Gallon jug with cap or cork

Have you ever wondered what makes ginger ale fizzy? All the little bubbles you see when you open a bottle of ginger ale are carbon dioxide —a gas that's in the air you breathe. Because bubbly drinks have carbon dioxide, they are often called *carbonated* drinks.

But how does the carbon dioxide get into the drink? The key is something called yeast. Yeast makes the differ-ence between "flat" water and fizzy soda. See the differ-ence for yourself when you mix water, yeast and flavorings to make your own ginger ale.

WHAT IS YEAST?

Yeasts are tiny, living plants. They are not active in your refrigerator because the cold keeps them in hibernation. But when you put them in a warm, moist place and give them sugar to eat, they get ac-tive and make carbon dioxide gas. This gas can make bread rise or drinks fizzy.

You can put a little yeast into a closed jug with warm, sugary water. As long as the yeast have enough sugar to eat, they'll keep making car-bon dioxide. When the air space above the water fills with carbon dioxide, the gas bubbles can't escape and they stay in the water. This makes the water carbonated. If the cap is loose, all the car-bon dioxide will escape from the jug. You'll get "flat" ginger ale.

1 Boil the water in the pot. Add:
■ Three tablespoons ginger. Use powdered ginger from the grocery store spice section or pound fresh ginger root from the produce section.
■ Juice squeezed from one-half of a lime.
■ Two and one-half cups sugar. Mix it well with a spoon until the sugar dissolves.
■ Three tablespoons cream of tartar. Mix well again.

2 Let the mixture cool to lukewarm. It is luke-warm when you put a drop on your wrist and it feels warm, but not hot. Ask your parents to show you how it is done. (Be careful. If the mixture is too hot, it will kill the yeast. It may also burn your wrist.) Once it's lukewarm, add 1 tablespoon baker's yeast and mix well. Cover the pot and let the mixture sit for six hours.

3 Now it is time to bottle your ginger ale. Start by straining it through a coffee filter or cheesecloth that's set into the top of a funnel. Some bits and pieces may slip through the cheese-cloth. That's okay. They will settle to the bottom. *Be sure to leave an air space at the top of the bottle to collect carbon dioxide.* Without the space, your jug may blow its top.

CHEESECLOTH

ONE GALLON JUG

FUNNEL

4 Once the ginger ale is in the jug, cap it tightly and put it into the refrig-erator. Make sure you keep your ginger ale in the refrigerator. If it's not kept cool, the yeast will be very active mak-ing carbon dioxide and alcohol. Alcohol may be fine in some adult drinks, but it is not fine in ginger ale. It will give your ginger ale an unpleasant flavor.

5 You can drink your ginger ale right away, but it will taste better if you wait two days. When you take your ginger ale out of the refrigerator, look for the bubbles.

Watch them rise to the surface and release their carbon dioxide. *Slowly* unscrew the top of the jug. Listen for a slow fizzle and then a POP! when the gas escapes from the jug. What does your brew smell like? More important, how does it taste?

VARIATIONS

■ Give your ginger ale even more flavor by adding a cup of fresh, chopped mint leaves when you put the ginger in. Then just strain them out with the ginger.

■ Try using honey to replace the sugar called for in the experiment.

■ For another taste treat, add your homemade ginger ale to lemonade or fruit juices. Make up your own variations. With homemade ginger ale, creativity is always in good taste.

AFTERWORDS

Yeasts are very tiny plants. They are related to mushrooms, molds, and other fungi. Like other fungi, yeasts can't produce their own food. To get energy, yeasts must first break down sugars and other carbohydrates.

Yeasts take in sugar, a molecule high in energy, and break it down into carbon dioxide and alcohol. This process is called fermentation. Yeasts use the energy released from this breakdown to support their own life processes. A similar reaction occurs when campers set fire to a pile of wood to release heat.

Through research and breeding experiments scientists have learned to produce yeasts that can make especially large amounts of carbon dioxide and yeasts that can make especially large amounts of alcohol.

Bakers take advantage of yeast that makes high levels of carbon dioxide in breadmaking. The gas bubbles that the baker's yeast gives off makes bread dough rise.

To make wine and beer, brewers use a yeast that produces high levels of alcohol. Since early times, brewer's yeast has also been used to cure various illnesses. It contains large amounts of B-complex vitamins that can be used by people. Baker's yeast does not.

The carbonation in your family's ginger ale results from the same reaction that occurs in your homemade bread or biscuits. Baker's yeast creates carbon dioxide that makes the bread dough rise. In the case of your ginger ale, the bottle cap keeps the carbon dioxide bubbles from escaping. They stay in the ginger ale solution, giving it that carbonated fizz.

Commercially made ginger ale goes through a different process. Instead of letting yeast make carbon dioxide bubbles, ginger ale manufacturers pump carbon dioxide into the ginger ale solution. The whole process is done under pressure, so that the gas bubbles are forced into the solution. The end product is the same—a fizzle when you open the bottle and bubbles of carbon dioxide you swallow when you drink ginger ale.

Yeasts contribute to the production of several other commercial food products. When fermentation is allowed to occur in the presence of oxygen, the yeast produces vinegar instead of alcohol. A poorly sealed bottle of wine may let oxygen into it, causing the wine to turn to vinegar. In the past, bacterial invasions into yeast doughs have resulted in new bread varieties. For instance, both rye and sourdough breads are made with a special "starter." The starter consists of the yeast dough combined with unique bacteria that gives a distinct flavor to each of these breads.

KARATE CHOP VEGGIES

KARATE CHOP VEGGIES

Hiiiiiiiiyaa! Karate-chop your veggies and watch them grow. You don't have to be a karate expert or own a samurai sword. All you need is 15 minutes to set up this experiment—and earn a Black Belt in indoor gardening!

YOU WILL NEED

Several root vegetables such as carrots, beets, turnips, parsnips, radishes, and rutabagas
Knife
Pebbles or gravel
Several shallow bowls
1 Very large carrot
Heavy string or twine
2 Sweet potatoes
2 Empty jars or large glasses
Toothpicks

Is there food in the roots of a plant? There must be, because carrots, radishes, and beets are all roots that we eat. They have sugar and starch in them. If people can use that food as fuel or energy, then maybe the plants can use it too. Find out how much energy is available by growing Karate Chop Veggies this month.

1 Look at several root vegetables, such as carrots, beets, turnips, parsnips, and radishes. Which side do you think is "up" when they are in the ground? Which is the top? Figure out where the leaves come out on each vegetable. That is the growing tip. If there are leaves already growing on the veggies, re-move them without cutting into the growing tip. With a knife (you might ask an adult to help you), chop off the bottoms of the root vegeta-bles, leaving only about 1" or 2" of vegetable below the growing tip. (Save the vege-table bottoms to use in the Root-a-Bake recipe shown below.)

2 Choose several shal-low bowls to grow your Karate Chop Veg-gies in. Put a layer of peb-bles or gravel in each bowl.

Set one vegetable top in each bowl, pushing the cut end down into the gravel to anchor it. Keep each bowl filled with ½" of water. New leaves should grow out of the top.

3 Will leaves grow up-side down? Find out by making a hanging carrot basket. Use a very large, fat carrot. Cut off the bottom half, leaving about 5" of the fattest part, including the top. Hold the carrot cut-side up and hollow out a section big enough to hold some water. The widest part of the carrot—the growing tip—will be on the bottom. Make a rope hanger for the carrot using two pieces of twine or heavy string. Tie the strings together in the middle and then pull them up around the carrot, as shown. Hang the carrot basket from a hook or a bent coat hanger, near a window. Fill hollowed-out section with water. The leaves should sprout out of the bottom. But will they grow *down*?

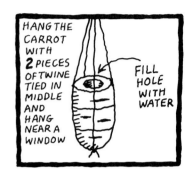

HANG THE CARROT WITH **2** PIECES OF TWINE TIED IN MIDDLE AND HANG NEAR A WINDOW

FILL HOLE WITH WATER

4 Which end is "up" on a sweet potato? Where will the leaves grow from? Look at two sweet potatoes. One end is more round than the other. One end has more of "scab" or scar than the other. Plant each sweet potato in a jar or glass of water to find out which end is the root. Plant one with the round end down. Plant the other with the round end up. Stick three toothpicks into the sides of the sweet potato as "arms" to support it in the glass. Keep the bottom third of the sweet potato covered with water. Set both jars in a warm, dark place until roots are formed. Then give the plants a little light, gradually. After a few days, you can place the sweet potatoes near a window for full light. When the sweet potato has sprouted many leaves, you can transfer it to a pot or the garden.

VARIATIONS

■ Chop off the top of a pineapple and grow it in pebbles or soil. If you use only pebbles and water, the leaves will continue to grow for a week or more. In soil, you can start a whole new plant.

■ Cut a potato into several pieces. Make sure that each piece has an "eye." Plant each piece in a separate pot of soil or in the garden.

1/2 in = 1.27 cm
1 in = 2.54 cm
2 in = 5.1 cm
3 in = 7.62 cm
5 in = 12.7 cm
1/4 C = .06 l
37 ft = 11.3 m
60 ft = 18.3 m
350° F = 176.6° C

ROOT-A-BAKE

2 Large carrots
2 Large parsnips
1 Large turnip
3 Tablespoons butter
¼ Cup brown sugar
Salt and pepper

CARROT

RADISH

BUTTER

PARSNIP

TURNIP

BEET

ST/88

23

Preheat oven to 350°. Use the vegetables above or use the leftover bottom parts of your Karate Chop Veggies; any combination of root vegetables will do. Cut the vegetables into sticks about 3" by ½". Cook 10 minutes, or until tender, in boiling water. Drain. Butter a small, shallow baking dish and arrange the vegetables in it. Sprinkle brown sugar over them and dot with more butter. Add salt and pepper to taste. Bake at 350° for 20 to 25 minutes, until the brown sugar and butter form a glaze.

AFTERWORDS

Have you ever seen a carrot flower? Probably not, and neither have most of the farmers who grow acres and acres of carrots each year. But carrots *do* have flowers and they do bear fruit. The problem is: They are *biennial* plants, which means that it takes them two years to complete their growing cycle. They don't flower until the second year. And since carrots are grown mainly for the edible root, they are pulled up out of the ground after just one growing season, before the flower ever has a chance to develop.

Turnips, rutabagas, parsnips, and beets are also biennial plants. But in most cases, these vegetables too are harvested after only a few months of growth. Usually these plants are grown for their roots, which store up large amounts of starch and sometimes sugar. The leaves of the young plants are small, and the stems are short. If harvested early, these plants become food for people. But if they are allowed to remain in the ground for another year, all of the food stored in these plants is then put to use by the plants themselves, and the stored starch is used to produce more leaves on a taller stem. In your Karate Chop activity, you coaxed the vegetables into using up the food stored in the root to produce more leaves. If the carrot had remained in the ground, it would have produced more leaves and even a flower or two.

Most root vegetables are grown just for the root, but turnips are an exception. In the South, many people eat the turnip greens—the leaves from the top of the plant—and throw the root away! In other parts of the country, people eat the root and throw the turnip tops away!

Red beets are grown for the root, but another beet is grown mostly for its green top, called Swiss chard. A third kind of beet is one that you probably eat almost every day. You sprinkle this root on your cereal. You bake cookies and cakes with this root. Can you guess what it is? It's the sugar beet, from which much of the world's sugar is made. In fact, the sugar in sugar beets is identical to the sugar in sugar cane. Both form a crystalline sugar when the juice is extracted from the plant.

Is a white potato a root? No, although sweet potatoes are. White potatoes are called *tubers* and they are actually underground stems. Each "eye" on the potato is like a bud on a twig. That's why farmers are able to cut up potatoes into several small pieces and plant the pieces to start new potato plants. As long as each piece has an eye, or bud, the potato will grow new leaves and more tubers.

Although quite a few roots are edible, most plants do not store food in their roots. In most plants, the roots are mainly an anchor for the plant and a system for carrying water and minerals to the stem. And the bigger the plant, the bigger the root system must be. Some trees have lateral root systems, spreading out horizontally, that are almost twice as wide as the tree is tall. A 37-foot-tall oak might have roots reaching out 60 feet from the base of the tree! A good rule of thumb is that the roots usually extend farther than the branches do. So next time you're standing under a large tree, look at the spread of the branches. Then walk just until you are no longer under the tree. More likely than not, there are roots under your feet!

GREASY KID STUFF

GREASY KID STUFF

1/4 lb= 113 g

Even if you don't like steak, french fries, or butter, you may be living off the fat of the land. Find out which foods are high in fat content by doing two easy kitchen experiments. You'll burn 110 calories of fuel or fat in the one hour it takes to complete this activity.

YOU WILL NEED

Brown paper bag
Various test foods such as:
butter, banana, apple, hard-boiled egg, uncooked frankfurter, potato, avocado, tomato, cottage cheese, cookies, nuts, cola, orange, lima beans, peanut butter, potato chips, etc.
Pen or felt marker

Have you heard all about the four food groups and their role in planning a healthy, well-balanced diet? If so, you know that you should eat Fruits and Vegetables, Milk and Dairy Foods, Meats / Fish / Poultry / Dried Beans, and Breads and Cereals every day. But there's another rule about nutrition that is just as impor-

tant for good health, and that is the rule about fats in your diet. Health experts suggest that no more than 30% to 35% of the calories you eat should come from fats.

But before you can plan a healthy, low-fat meal, you need to find out which foods are high in fats, and which foods are not. Greasy Kid Stuff will help you sort out the "fat" foods from the other ones!

DEFINITIONS

Calorie: This is a unit of measure that refers to the amount of heat or energy a food will produce. Different foods will produce different amounts of energy. Ounce for ounce, fats will produce a lot more heat or energy than proteins or carbohydrates, and so fats are high in calories.

Carbohydrates: Almost all carbohydrates come from plants. There are two main kinds of foods in the carbohydrates group — sugars and starches. Peaches and berries are sugary carbohydrates, while peas and potatoes are starchy carbohydrates. Wheat,

rice, and the other grains are primarily starch as well.

Protein: Every living cell contains protein, which is why meats, fish, and poultry are such good sources of this important kind of food. Milk and dairy products are also very rich in protein, and so are dried peas and beans. Protein's main job is to help the body grow.

Fats: The oily or greasy part of meat, poultry, fish, nuts, seeds, and so on.

1 Cut open a large brown paper bag and lay it flat. This will be your Fats Chart. Cut off a small pat of butter and rub it on at the top of the paper-bag chart, until the butter stains. Write the word "Butter" under the stain, and put a number 10 beside it. Butter will make the greasiest stain, since it is almost *all* fat.

2 Next, look at all of the foods you're going to test, and try to decide which one has the *least* fat in it. Rub that food on the bag

near the bottom. Write the name of the food underneath the stain it makes, and put a number 1 beside it.

3 Now try to decide where the other test foods fit in the scale from 1 to 10. If you think peaches are very fatty, put them near the top of the chart and give them a high number. Continue testing foods for fat by rubbing each food on the bag and numbering the stains. With dry foods like cookies, you may want to warm them in your hands first, and then rub hard to make a mark. Label each stain by writing the name of the food underneath it.

4 Look at the bag a few hours later — or the next day — when the wet stains have dried. Hold the bag up to the light and you will see a greasy, see-through mark by each food that contains fat. The more fat in the food, the greasier the stain will be. Did you put all of the foods in the right order? If so, you will have a column of stains that goes from very greasy to not greasy at all. If you find a big greasy mark near the bottom of your scale, or a "blank" space near the top, you guessed wrong about the fat content of the foods!

Does the mark from the banana surprise you? How about the stain above the word cheese? Did you know that many nutritious foods are very high in fat?

HOW TO LOSE FAT—FAST!
When it comes to cooking hamburgers, there's a great way to cut your own fat intake. It's called *broiling.* Find out how much fat you can lose — from a hamburger patty, that is — by trying this dinner-time experiment.

■ Divide a pound of ground beef into four hamburger patties, each weighing about ¼ pound. Try to make the patties as equal in size as possible.

■ Fry two of the hamburgers in a skillet on top of the stove.

Broil two of them in a broiler pan in the oven.

■ When the hamburgers are cooked, look in the pans to see how much fat they've lost. Which cooking method removed the most fat from the hamburgers? Measure the fat in the broiler by scooping it out a tablespoon at a time.

Then do the same with the fat in the frying pan — if there is any! If there *isn't* any fat in the frying pan, where is it?

■ Did you know that most butcher shops and meat departments add chunks of white fat to the beef before grinding it into hamburger? By law, hamburger may contain

27

as much as 30% added fat. That's in addition to the fat that is already present in the red part of the meat!

VARIATIONS

■ Go on a Supermarket Safari looking for fats! Read the ingredients labels on cookies, crackers, cakes, frozen doughnuts, breakfast cereals, etc. You'll be surprised how many dessert foods contain beef fat or other animal fats. Next, read and compare the nutrition information labels on many different foods. Make a chart showing how many grams of fat there are in a single serving of whole milk, low-fat milk, cottage cheese, one pat of butter, various canned soups, frozen dinners, potato chips, breads, and so on.

■ Which foods are most satisfying? Eat a meal that is entirely fat-free. You may want to consult your brown bag chart of grease stains and your Supermarket Safari list to help you decide what your fat-free meal should have in it. After your fat-free meal, how long is it until you are hungry again? The next day, eat a starch-free meal and make a note of when your hunger pangs return.

AFTERWORDS

Fats have fallen into disfavor recently, especially among people who are concerned about heart disease and good health. Nevertheless, fats are a necessary and important part of any diet. For one thing, fats provide a good source of energy. They also slow down the rate of digestion, which means that you will feel "satisfied" longer after eating a high-fat meal. Fats carry the fat-soluble vitamins A, D, E, and K; these vitamins can be dissolved only in fat and not in water like the other vitamins. And lastly, many fats contain an essential nutrient, linoleic acid, that is necessary for normal growth and healthy skin.

The problem is that most Americans eat *too many* fats. Since the early 1900s, American consumption of fat has risen 25%, while consumption of carbohydrates has fallen by the same amount. This trend is probably an unhealthy one, because there seems to be a connection between the amount of saturated fat you eat and your chance of getting heart disease and certain kinds of cancer. For this reason, many nutrition experts recommend that fats account for no

more than 30% to 35% of the calories consumed daily. The average American diet, however, currently contains about 45% fat.

In any plan to reduce fats in your diet, the key word is *saturated*. Saturated fats are thought to contain larger amounts of cholesterol than polyunsaturated fats. And although the question of cholesterol levels is still being debated, many doctors suggest that people with a history of high blood pressure and/or heart disease should cut down on high-cholesterol foods.

But how do you know which fats are saturated and which fats are not? Here are some easy guidelines to help you answer that question. Saturated fats are usually solid at room temperature, and they come primarily from animal sources — meat, milk and dairy products, and eggs. *Polyunsaturated* fats, on the other hand, are usually liquid at room temperature. They come from vegetable sources — safflower oil and corn oil are two examples — and they are thought to help *decrease*

the level of cholesterol in the blood. The two *monounsaturated* fats, olive oil and peanut oil, also have a positive effect on cholesterol levels.

For people who want to cut down on cholesterol, it's animal fats that must be eliminated. This can mean switching from butter to margarine, cutting down on the number of eggs eaten each week, choosing skim milk instead of whole milk at mealtimes, and eating leaner cuts of meat.

But in any discussion of nutrition it's important to remember that no single nutrient should be completely eliminated from the diet. Cholesterol is a good example of this rule. In fact, cholesterol is needed by the body for digestion and for the formation of hormones and vitamin D. Your body can probably manufacture all the cholesterol you need. But it would still be a mistake to cut out all foods that contain cholesterol, because many of those foods provide *other* valuable nutrients that are of great importance in a well-balanced diet.

ICE CREAM MACHINE

ICE CREAM MACHINE

Which is colder: ice or ice cream? You'll find out when you get the scoop on the amazing Ice-Cream Machine! From mixing to tasting should take about 45 minutes.

YOU WILL NEED

Empty coffee can with plastic lid
Scissors
Wooden spoon
Ingredients for Vanilla Cookie Ice Cream (see box)
Bowl
Electric mixer
5-Pound bag of ice
Brown grocery bag
Hammer
Newspapers
Bucket
2 to 2½ Cups table salt
Empty plastic container or ice-cube tray

Homemade ice cream and clear roads during a winter blizzard—what do these two things have in common? They

both depend on the special relationship between ice and salt. Salt melts ice: That's why it's spread on icy roads in the winter. But salt also causes the temperature of water to go down. You'll use salt to melt ice and lower the temperature of the water in your Ice-Cream Machine. Believe it or not, the water will get colder than 32 degrees Fahrenheit—but it won't freeze! Pretty cool, huh?

INGREDIENTS FOR VANILLA COOKIE ICE CREAM

(adapted from a recipe published in *Consumer Reports* magazine)

1 Egg
⅔ Cup sugar
1 Teaspoon vanilla
1 Cup heavy cream
2 Cups half-and-half
¾ Cup of your favorite cookies, crushed by hand

1 Before you begin, have ready all the ingredients for Vanilla Cookie Ice Cream and all of the equipment listed. Wash and dry the empty coffee can and lid. Using a scissors, poke a small hole in the plastic lid. Make sure the hole is *off-center*. Enlarge the hole by pushing the wooden-spoon handle through the hole. Don't make the hole *too* big: The spoon handle should fit tightly in the hole. With the scissors, trim away the rough edges of plastic around the hole.

2 Make the ice-cream mix by putting the egg, sugar, and vanilla into a bowl and beating with an electric mixer for 1 minute on a medium speed. Add the cream and half-and-half, and mix on low speed for 3 minutes. (You'll add the crushed cookies later.) Set the ice-cream mix back in the refrigerator until your bucket of ice is ready to go.

3 Now you need to make crushed ice. Put the 5-pound bag of ice inside a brown grocery bag, fold the bag end closed, and pound the ice with a hammer on the kitchen floor. It might help to cover the grocery bag with a layer of newspapers, to keep the hammer from breaking through the paper bag. Pour about one-third of the crushed ice into the bucket. Cover the ice with about ½ cup of salt. Put the coffee can on top of the ice, in the middle of the bucket. Add ice and salt in layers around the can until you have used up all of the ice. **But don't use all of the salt**

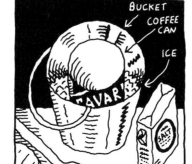

yet. You may not need it all, or you may need to add some later.

4 Pour about two-thirds of the ice-cream mix into the coffee can. Pour the rest of the mix into a plastic container or empty ice-cube tray and stick it in the freezer right away. This part of your ice-cream experiment is what scientists call the "control": It gives you another method of freezing your mixture so you can compare and see which method works best. When you have finished making ice cream, immediately check the control portion in the freezer. Is it frozen yet? Can you figure out why?

5 Stick the wooden spoon into the coffee can with the ice-cream mix. Snap on the plastic lid, letting the spoon handle stick up through the hole. The wooden spoon has two jobs in your ice-cream machine: It's a handle for turning the can, and a *dasher* for stirring the ice cream. Now grab this handle and start turning the can. Every 2 or 3 minutes, stop spinning the can and hold it still so you can use the dasher (the "bowl" of the

wooden spoon) to stir the ingredients inside. Try to mix in as much air as you can: Move the dasher in a circular motion around the bottom of the can and the side. Don't remove the lid to do this.

After about 10 or 15 minutes of spinning the can, take the lid off and add the crushed cookies. Replace the lid and continue as before. You can check on your progress every once in a while, but don't take the lid off *too* often. You'll notice when you're stirring that the mixture is getting thicker. All together, it will probably take about 25 to 30 minutes to make ice cream. But don't worry: It's not hard work! You can keep the can spinning without much muscle power. And it never hurts to have a hungry friend handy, to help you take "turns"! **Remember:** When the ice cream is done, check the control portion in the freezer.

HINTS FOR SUCCESS:

■ Make sure all the ice-cream ingredients are cold when you start.

■ If the ice doesn't seem to be melting in the bottom of the bucket, add a small amount of water to get it going.

■ Don't add too much salt at first: You can always add more later if you need it. The more salt you use, the faster the ice will melt. If the ice melts too fast, ice crystals will form and the mix will harden too soon —before you have a chance to stir enough air into it. Air is what gives ice cream its smooth texture. Air also keeps you from noticing how *cold* the ice cream is! Is your home-made ice cream colder than store-bought ice cream? Which do you think is the most "airy"?

■ Be patient. At first, the ice cream may not seem to be solidifying, but after about 20 minutes, you'll notice the change.

```
5 lbs = 2.26 kg
1/2 C = .12 l
2/3 C = .16 l
3/4 C = .18 l
1 C = .24 l
2 C = .48 l
2 to 2 1/2 C = .48 to .6 l
32° F = 0° C
1 tsp = 5 ml
```

AFTERWORDS

Ice cream is the delicious result of some important scientific principles. No one knows for sure when ice cream was invented, but frozen desserts have been around for a long time. The Romans had fruit ices, and Marco Polo claims to have eaten some ice milk during his travels to the Far East.

If you've eaten ice milk or fruit ices, however, you know that they just aren't...well, as *creamy* as ice cream. So who put the creaminess in ice cream? Probably the Europeans. In the 1700s they discovered that salt could lower the temperature of ice—and that meant that frozen desserts could be frozen much more quickly. When milk and cream are frozen quickly, ice crystals don't have time to form.

In your ice-cream experiment, you probably found out that it's hard to get the perfect balance between freezing the mixture quickly enough so that ice crystals can't form, and freezing it slowly enough so that you have time to incorporate plenty of air. "Overrun" is what ice-cream manufacturers call the air that is mixed into ice cream. Using huge machines with gigantic dash-

ers, they can double the volume of ice cream by adding as much air as there is cream, sugar, and milk! Ice cream with a lot of overrun doesn't weigh very much, and it's pretty frothy in your mouth, too. But ice cream without air is too hard and too cold: It's more like frozen milk. The mixed-in air actually keeps you from noticing how cold the ice cream is!

To keep manufacturers from cheating the public by putting huge quantities of air into ice cream, the government requires that a gallon of ice cream weigh at least 4½ pounds. Next time you're in the grocery store, compare the less-expensive ice creams with the higher-priced ones. You can probably tell just by lifting them which ones are full of air. When you think about the fact that you're getting more *food* and less air in the heavier ice creams, doesn't it make the high price a little easier to swallow?

Modern-day manufacturers use huge freezers instead of salt and ice to freeze the ice cream ingredients. But before freezers were invented, people needed ice to make ice cream. Without refrigeration,

though, it was hard to get ice in the summer. Some people, who lived near rivers or lakes, had icehouses to store ice in, and they could make ice cream in the summer. In winter, they took huge chunks of ice from the river and packed the giant ice cubes in hay for insulation. The ice lasted for months that way—but by August, it was often melted. In those days, ice cream was eaten more often in December than in the good old summertime. Quite a chilly treat!

People often wonder how salt can *melt* snow and ice on the roads if it actually makes ice water *colder.* And if the melted ice is colder than 32 degrees, then why doesn't it freeze again right away? The answer is that as the ice melts, it dissolves the salt and makes saltwater. Saltwater doesn't freeze at 32 degrees the way plain water does: It freezes at a *lower* temperature.

Now that you're an expert about ice cream, you might want to go into the ice-cream business. Maybe you'll be the first person to come up with a flavor no one's ever thought of yet. What a sweet life! Just try not to lick up all your profits!

KITCHEN BOTANY

KITCHEN BOTANY

16 oz = 453 g
12 ft = 3.6 m

Kitchen Botany is a good activity to begin about an hour before dinner. After you are finished, eat the less sweet produce with a dip. Eat the sweet produce with fondue for dessert. Recipes are included.

YOU WILL NEED

At least one of the following from each group:
Cucumber, zucchini, watermelon
Apple, pear, quince
Tomato, grape, blueberry
Plum, cherry, peach
Carrot, celery, parsnip
Onion, garlic, shallot
Cabbage, cauliflower, broccoli
Cutting board
Knife
Magnifying glass (optional)
Ingredients for Dip and Fondue (optional)

Have you ever eaten a flower? What plant parts do you eat? A tomato is a vegetable—isn't it? This activity deals with fruit and vegetables you eat all the time. They will help you answer these questions. You'll take a look and then take a taste. And then you can grow your own garden with what's left over.

1 Put all of the produce on a table. Place all fruits in one pile and all vegetables in another. How did you decide which pile to put each piece in? Was your choice based on color or taste? Was it based on the section in which each can be found in a grocery? None of these things will help you separate the fruits from the vegetables. The following will.

2 Place a cutting board and knife on the table. Being careful with the knife (or ask an adult to help), cut each piece of produce in half crosswise.

3 Examine each half carefully. Use a magnifying glass if you have one. If you find seeds or pits inside, the piece of produce is a fruit. If there are no seeds, it is a vegetable. Reclassify, or regroup, your produce into separate piles of fruits and vegetables.

4 Eat the vegetables with a dip as an appetizer before dinner, or put them in the refrigerator for later use in cooking.

5 Line up the fruit on the table. Fruits come in all shapes and sizes. They can be mushy or crunchy, with seeds or with a pit. There are names that describe these

differences. Try to match each piece of fruit with its descriptive name.
■ Pepo (PEEP-o): a fleshy fruit with many seeds inside and a harder rind outside.
■ Pome (like ROME): a fruit with a hard covering around its seeds.
■ Berry: a pulpy fruit that has many seeds.
■ Drupe (DROOP): a fruit with a hard pit that covers one seed.

6 Refrigerate the fruits, or eat them for dessert with honey or cream or chocolate fondue. Save some seeds to grow your own houseplants.

FONDUE

Melt one package of chocolate chips in a double boiler. Ask an adult to show you how. Dip the fruit in it with forks.

If chocolate is something you avoid, serve the fruit with several kinds of cheese.

DIP

Mix one package of dried onion soup mix with one 16-ounce container of cultured sour cream. Chill before serving.

VARIATIONS

Some fruit seeds and vegetable parts can be used to grow beautiful plants.

■ Plant orange or other citrus seeds in potting soil and water them. Keep them in a warm place until seedlings develop, then move them to a sunny spot.

■ Apple, peach, pear, and plum seeds need a cold period before they will grow. Scratch the seeds with sandpaper and plant them in plant moss and keep them in the refrigerator for about two months. Then plant them in potting soil and watch them grow.

■ Make hanging planters from root vegetables such as carrots, beets, turnips, etc. Cut off the top two inches of the vegetable. Scoop out the core. Hang the plant upside down by putting toothpicks into the vegetable and hanging it with a string. Keep the scooped-out hole filled with water. You may have to fill it several times each day. Green leaves will grow out from the vegetable top, up and around your "planter."

AFTERWORDS

When you divided your produce into fruits and vegetables, you were *classifying* it. Classification is the act of sorting objects by certain rules, or criteria. When you sorted your produce, the criterion was that all produce with seeds is fruit. Classification is an important scientific tool. People who study plants know that plants with similar flowers, fruits, leaves, or growth forms are often related. Just like people, these related forms are grouped into families.

The squash family includes cucumbers, pumpkins, watermelons, cantaloupes, and gourds; it also includes summer squashes such as zucchini and winter squashes such as acorn. These fruits grow on vines with five-sided stems that creep along the ground or climb by wrapping their small tendrils around other plants, fences, etc. They have fairly large leaves, often shaped like maple leaves. We generally eat only the fleshy parts of the squash family fruits, but cucumber and zucchini are eaten flesh, seeds, rind and all. There are even recipes for fried squash blossoms and squash blossom soup in some cookbooks.

The tomato family is sometimes called the nightshade family. Some nightshades, like the deadly nightshade of Europe, are extremely poisonous. Its more tasty family members include tomatoes, potatoes, peppers, and eggplant. Appropriately, tobacco also comes from this family. Members of this family usually have flowers with five petals and fruit in either a pod or berry with many seeds.

The rose family includes apples, cherries, strawberries, pears, plums, almonds, and peaches. Members of the rose family can be as small as a rosebush or as large as a tree. Their flowers commonly have five rounded petals. Rose hips, high in vitamin C and often used in herbal teas, are the fruit of a rose flower much like the ones seen in gardens. In ancient times, the rose was used medically. It was a favorite of the Romans, who spread its culture wherever their armies conquered.

Vegetables are also classified into families. Members of the mustard family include broccoli, cauliflower, cabbage, radishes, turnips, brussels sprouts, kale, horseradish, and mustard plants. Members of the mustard family are sometimes called crucifers (KROOS-i-ferz), from their Latin name, which describes the crossshape of the four petals of the mustard flower. The mustard that we spread on sandwiches is made from ground mustard seeds mixed with vinegar or oil and spices. While most mustard plants are fairly small, the black mustard plant of Palestine can grow up to 12 feet tall and have birds singing in its branches. Even a phenomenon like that does not defy classification.

SERIOUS LOAFING

SERIOUS LOAFING

100° F	= 37.7° C
115° F	= 46.1° C
375° F	= 190.5° C
400° F	= 204.4° C

Rise and shine! It's time to find out what makes bread rise. You'll need at least 4 hours to get from mixing to baking to eating. In the meantime, mmm-mmm—what a wonderful smell!

YOU WILL NEED

2 Large drinking glasses
2 Packages active dry yeast
1 Tablespoon sugar
All ingredients for Good White Bread, as listed in recipe
Large and small bowls
Measuring cups
Small saucepan
Wooden spoon (or hand-held or electric mixer)
Kitchen utensils
Plastic wrap
9" by 5" by 3" Loaf pan
Pot holders or oven mitts

EXPERIMENTING WITH YEAST

What does yeast actually do and how does it make bread rise? To find out, try this easy experiment. In a large drinking glass, mix 1 package of active dry yeast and ½ cup

of *very* warm water (100° to 115°F.). Label this YEAST. Stir well to dissolve the yeast. In another glass, mix 1 package active dry yeast, ½ cup very warm water, *and* 1 tablespoon sugar. Stir well. Label this YEAST AND SUGAR. Set both glasses in a warm spot and watch what happens. Within 10 or 15 minutes, you will know which yeast mixture is producing a gas called *carbon dioxide*. That gas is what makes bread rise. Keep this experiment for several hours and watch to see how long the yeast keeps on working, making carbon dioxide bubbles. What happens when the yeast runs out of gas?

MAKING BREAD

1 Make sure that you have permission to use your stove and oven. You may need an adult's help. Take the middle rack out of the oven. Preheat oven to 400° (375° if you are using a glass baking pan) and assemble all the ingredients

for the Good White Bread recipe.

INGREDIENTS FOR GOOD WHITE BREAD

1 Package active dry yeast*
½ Cup very warm water (100° to 115°F.)
2 Tablespoons sugar
4 Tablespoons (½ stick) melted butter
1½ Cups warm milk
1 Tablespoon salt
5 to 6 Cups unbleached or bread flour
*For an even fluffier loaf, try 2 packages of yeast.

In a small bowl, combine the 1 package active dry yeast and ½ cup very warm water. The water should be 100° to 115°—it will feel quite warm but not burning hot to your fingers. Stir well. When the yeast is mostly dissolved, add 2 tablespoons sugar. "Proof" the yeast by letting the mixture sit for 5 to 10 minutes. It will start to bubble and foam like your yeast-and-sugar experiment. If it doesn't foam up,

either the water is too hot or the yeast isn't fresh.

2 While the yeast is proofing, melt 4 tablespoons butter and add it to 1½ cups warm milk. Stir in 1 tablespoon salt. Now you will begin adding flour. All together, you will probably need 5 or 6 cups flour, or more. Start by adding 3 cups flour to the milk-and-butter mixture, and stir with a wooden spoon, or with a hand-held or electric mixer. Then add the yeast mixture to the dough and mix well for 1 minute. Add 2 more cups of flour, or enough to make the dough pull away from the sides of the bowl. You may need to add all of the flour. The dough should not be too sticky because in the next step you are going to knead it.

3 Turn the dough out of the bowl onto a floured board or floured countertop and knead it until it is smooth and elastic—for about 5 to

10 minutes. To knead the dough, push into the dough with your fist or with the heel of your hand. Then fold the sides of the dough over and repeat the process. Turn the dough frequently as you knead it. Keep adding flour to the board and to the dough if the dough gets too sticky. When the dough is smooth and elastic, divide it into two equal pieces. Put half the dough in a clean, buttered bowl. Turn it over once or twice to coat it with butter. Cover dough with plastic wrap and let it rise in a warm place until it is double in bulk—twice its original size. This may take from 1 to 2 hours. Check it frequently.

4 In the meantime, butter the inside of a 9" by 5" by 3" loaf pan. Put the other half of the dough into the loaf pan and brush the top with water. Bake it immediately—*without letting it rise*—on the lowest rack in a 400° oven (375° if your loaf pan is glass). Bake for 40 minutes and then check it by carefully knocking on the bread. (Use pot holders to pull the pan from the oven.) If the bread sounds hollow, it's probably done. You should also carefully turn the loaf out of the pan and knock on the bottom, to make sure it sounds hollow too. Allow the bread to cool on a rack, and then slice it and try it. Even though it hasn't risen much, you can still eat it. How does it taste?

5 Wash the loaf pan and butter the insides again. Now check on the dough in the bowl. When it has doubled in bulk, punch it down. How long did it take for the bread to

rise? Is it more or less time than it took for your yeast-and-sugar experiment to fill the glass with foam? Turn the dough out of the bowl and knead it again for 3 or 4 minutes. Shape it into a loaf and put it in the buttered pan. Cover with plastic wrap. *Allow it to rise a second time, until it is double in bulk.* Brush the top with water. Bake it on the lower rack in a 400° oven (375° for glass pans) for 40 to 45 minutes. Knock on the loaf, as in Step 4, to see if it's done.

Most bakers say that bread should cool completely before you slice it. But who can resist hot, freshly baked bread? How does it taste, compared with the first loaf of bread that was not allowed to rise?

AFTERWORDS

Yeast is a microscopic plant that can change sugar into carbon dioxide and alcohol. This process is called *fermentation.* In your first experiment, the yeast converted the sugar-water to carbon dioxide, and you saw the glass fill up with foam. The foam is actually many tiny bubbles of carbon dioxide gas. Carbon dioxide is the colorless and odorless gas we exhale when we breathe.

The rising of bread is simply like blowing up a million tiny balloons scattered throughout the dough—except that *you* don't blow up the balloons. The yeast does. To make bread rise, you must give the yeast some sugar, and you must distribute the yeast throughout the bread dough by kneading it. Otherwise the bread will rise in some places and not in others. Did you find a few large holes in your loaf of bread? If so, you probably didn't knead it enough. Holes in a loaf of bread mean that larger patches of yeast were gathered there, giving off a whole lot of carbon dioxide.

But why does yeast give off carbon dioxide in the first place? Because yeast is a living plant and it behaves like all living cells. It uses oxygen to maintain life. When you take in oxygen and give off carbon dioxide, the process is called *respiration.* Even dandelions use oxygen from the environment and then give off carbon dioxide as waste material. So why can't we use dandelions to make bread?

The answer is that most plants, including dandelions, use up the carbon dioxide they produce in a process called *photosynthesis*—the making of food for the plant. Dandelions make their own sugar—they don't need a glass of sugar-water to help them grow. And the carbon dioxide produced by the dandelion is used right away by the dandelion itself. Yeasts, on the other hand, are not green plants and do not make their own food. They feed on other plants and animals. So the carbon dioxide they produce is not needed for photosynthesis. It is not used up and it can be seen as bubbles in the glass. It can also be used to make bread rise.

Another byproduct of yeast's respiration is alcohol. Alcohol is produced quickly and in large amounts when yeast is combined with sugar in a *low-oxygen* environment. When wine and beer are made, the yeast is not *aerated*—not allowed to get much oxygen—and consequently more alcohol is produced. Very little alcohol was produced by the yeasts in your bread recipe, because so much air was present when you were mixing and kneading the dough. Any alcohol produced was burned off during baking.

Yeast is what makes beer alcoholic, and the carbon dioxide from the yeast gives the beer its carbonated or fizzy taste. Some bread recipes even call for a can of beer, instead of yeast, to make the dough rise! Again, the alcohol in the beer burns off when the bread is baked.

Yeasts are in the air and often settle on foods that are left uncovered or unrefrigerated. Then the yeasts go to work converting the sugars in the food into carbon dioxide and alcohol. If you've ever left a jug of apple cider, tightly closed, in the refrigerator for too long, it probably became alcoholic-tasting. Yeast strikes again!

1 T = 15 ml	1/2 C = .12 l
2 T = 30 ml	1 1/2 C = .36 l
4 T = 60 ml	2 C = .48 l
3 in = 7.6 cm	3 C = .72 l
5 in = 12.7 cm	5 C = 1.2 l
9 in = 22.9 cm	6 C = 1.4 l

YUMMY YOGURT

YUMMY YOGURT

1 in = 2.54 cm	1/2 tsp = 2.5 ml
6 in = 15.2 cm	1 tsp = 5 ml
1 qt = .95 l	2 tsp = 10 ml
8 oz = 240 ml	1 T = 15 ml
	2 T = 30 ml

What's white and sour and comes with fruit on the bottom? A grouchy polar bear who's been tramping around in a cherry orchard! Or maybe the answer is yogurt—which you can make yourself. In that case, it's not quite so sour and it comes with fruit on the top! Allow about 45 minutes to make a yogurt warming box, and one hour more to prepare the yogurt itself. It will take 7 to 8 hours for the yogurt to "cure."

YOU WILL NEED
Small cardboard box, or
    insulated food cooler
6-Inch stack of newspapers
6 Plastic trash bags
1 Quart fresh whole milk
Saucepan
Candy thermometer
4 8-ounce cups or jars
Measuring spoons
Small bowl
2 Teaspoons fresh plain
    yogurt (check expiration
    dates for freshness)
Aluminum foil
Masking tape, pen or marker

What's the difference between yogurt and milk? Just one thing: bacteria. Yogurt is made with bacteria that grow and multiply and cause the milk to "set" into a custardy, creamy, delicious food. You can make your own yogurt for less than half the price of commercial yogurt—and all you need is a little culture to get you started!

1 To make yogurt, you will first need to make an insulated "warming box" to keep the bacteria happy. Start with a small cardboard box from the grocery store, or use an insulated food cooler. Line the bottom and the four sides of the box each with a stack of newspapers at least 1" thick. You may want to enclose each stack of newspapers in a clean plastic garbage bag, to keep everything dry and clean. Make a sixth pack of newspapers 1" thick, wrapped in a plastic bag, to use as a lid. If you are using a food cooler, add some newspapers anyway, as extra insulation. Try to leave just enough space inside the warming box for the number of cups or jars you plan to use.

2 Place the insulated box in a spot where it can remain undisturbed for the next 8 hours. Have the clean cups or jars ready nearby. Heat 1 quart of fresh milk (don't use old or sour milk) slowly in a large saucepan until it reaches 180°F on the candy thermometer. Pour the milk into the cups or jars, and set them close together in the warming box. Do not fill the jars all the way to the top— leave about an inch of room at the top. Place the candy thermometer in one of the jars and check it every few minutes. When the milk in the jars has cooled to 110°F, it's time to add the yogurt starter. It may take 30 to 45 minutes for the milk to cool to this point.

3 Now you must work quickly. Take 1 tablespoon of milk from each pint of milk you are using. If you started with 1 quart of milk, you will need to take a total of 2 tablespoons of milk from the jars. It's okay to take 1 tablespoon from each of two jars, and forget about the other two jars for the moment. Put the 2 tablespoons of warm milk— 110°F in a small bowl and add 2 teaspoons of fresh plain yogurt. This is called adding the "culture." Don't use any more than 1 teaspoon of yogurt for each tablespoon of warm milk. Stir it up gently. Now divide this mixture evenly among *all four jars* of warm milk in the insulated box. Gently stir, to mix the yogurt culture in well. Cover the jars if you have lids. Place a sheet of aluminum foil on top of the jars, as an extra cover. Put the top layer of newspaper insulation on as a lid.

4 Leave the jars in the warming box undisturbed for 6 to 8 hours. Then check the yogurt. If it has set, put it in the refrigerator to cool. If the yogurt does not set within 8 hours, see the Trouble Spots list.

110° F	= 43° C
115° F	= 46° C
120° F	= 49° C
150° F	= 66° C
180° F	= 82° C

TROUBLE SPOTS

■ Was the plain yogurt starter too old—past its expiration date?

■ Was the milk too hot— warmer than 110°F—when you added the starter?

■ Did you jiggle or open the warming box too much during the eight hours?

VARIATIONS

■ Find out what happens to the bacteria in your yogurt starter by adding it while the milk is still hot—hotter than 110°F. You can set up a controlled experiment with four cups of milk. With masking tape and a pen, label one cup "Plain—no starter." Don't add any starter to this jar. Label the other three jars with the temperature that the milk was when you added the starter. Try adding ½ teaspoon plain yogurt starter to 8 ounces of hot milk while it is still 180°F. In another jar, add the ½ teaspoon of starter when the milk is 150°F. In the fourth jar, add the starter when the milk is almost cool enough, say about 115 to 120°F. Let all four jars sit in the insulated box. Begin checking the samples after four hours. Did the yogurt made with hotter milk set more quickly? How does it taste compared to the yogurt made with cooler milk?

■ Try adding a little more starter yogurt—1 or 2 teaspoons per cup of milk—to see how it affects the taste.

■ Add 1 or 2 tablespoons of powdered milk to make a thicker, firmer yogurt.

JAM TIME

If you like your yogurt with sweetened fruit, try adding a few tablespoons of strawberry jam or peach preserves to the homemade yogurt. Mix well and enjoy!

AFTERWORDS

Making yogurt might seem like magic to someone who doesn't understand bacteria. After all, you simply heat up some milk, add a tiny bit of yogurt and—poof!—you've got *more* yogurt! It would be great if you could do that with chocolate.

But yogurt has a secret ingredient: bacteria. When the right kind of bacteria are introduced to a container of warm milk, they begin to "feed" on the *lactose,* or milk sugar. They use the lactose as a source of energy, and change it into lactic acid. That's why yogurt is sour, while milk is almost sweet. As the milk becomes sour, the protein in the milk begins to break down and it *coagulates,* or sets. That's what makes the milk become firm, like a custard.

Usually two different kinds of bacteria are found in yogurt: *Lactobacillus bulgaricus* and *Streptococcus thermophilus.* These two bacteria really work well together; they stimulate each other's growth. But they don't both grow at the same time. *S. thermophilus* grows better at lower temperatures, while *L. bulgaricus* grows better at higher temperatures. If you introduced the yogurt starter while the milk was still quite warm, you probably produced a more sour- or tart-tasting yogurt. That's because *L. bulgaricus* took over; it produces more acid than *S. thermophilus* does.

What happened if you introduced the bacteria to the hot milk while it was still almost 180 degrees? You probably killed the bacteria! Most bacteria will be killed at that temperature, which is why you heated it in the first place. You didn't want to be growing other, possibly harmful kinds of bacteria while you were making your yogurt.

The sourness of yogurt depends almost entirely on which kind of bacteria are allowed to take over while the yogurt is fermenting. To make a mild, creamy yogurt that isn't too tart, you need to encourage the *S. thermophilus* to grow. Of course, some of that bacteria must be present in your starter to begin with. The problem is that *S. thermophilus* doesn't live too long in the refrigerator, so if your yogurt starter isn't fresh, the bacteria probably aren't there.

Yogurt has the reputation for being a healthy food—and it is. Basically, it has the same nutritional value as the milk it was made from, but yogurt is easier to digest. The fermentation process—the process of changing milk sugar into lactic acid—helps to partially digest some of the protein in milk. Yogurt and milk are also both very high in calcium, which is necessary for your bones and teeth. But in order for your body to use calcium, it must be absorbed in an acid environment. Only about 20% to 30% of the calcium in milk can be absorbed by your body. Since yogurt is acidic on its own, the calcium in yogurt can be absorbed more easily.

Yogurt is believed to be one of the oldest foods in the world—and it is eaten by some of the oldest people in the world. People from the Balkan countries are known for eating a lot of yogurt, and many of them live to be 100 years old! Maybe the yogurt contributes to their longevity, or perhaps some other factors are responsible. Enjoy your homemade yogurt, even if you don't live to be 110!

FOR MORE INFORMATION . . .

Places to Write and Visit

Here are some places you can write or visit for more information about food and the kitchen. When you write, include your name and address, and be specific in your questions. Don't forget to enclose a stamped, self-addressed envelope for a reply.

Children's Nutrition Research Center
U.S. Department of Agriculture
Baylor College of Medicine
6608 Fannin
Medical Towers Building, Suite 601
Houston, TX 77030

Human Nutrition Information Services
U.S. Department of Agriculture
6505 Belcrest Road
Hyattsville, MD 20782

Exploratorium
Palace of Arts and Sciences
3601 Lyon Street
San Francisco, CA 94123

Fats and Proteins Research Foundation
2250 E. Devon Avenue
Des Plaines, IL 60018

Kansas Health Museum
309 Main Street
Halstead, KS 67056

Further Reading about Food and the Kitchen

Here are more books you can read about food and the kitchen. Check your local library or bookstore to see if they have the books or can order them for you.

Creative Food Experiences for Children. Goodman and Pollen (Center for Science in the Public Interest)
Junk Food. What It Is, What It Does. Seixas (Greenwillow)
Knead It, Pinch It, Bake It! Jones and Jones (Crowell Jr.)
Night Markets. Bringing Food to a City. Horwitz (Harper Collins)
Pizza. Fischer (Watts)
Slumps, Grunts, and Snickerdoodles. What Colonial America Ate and Why. Perl (Houghton Mifflin)
Sugarbush. Making Maple Syrup (Hillsdale Educational)
Wild Edibles. Hamilton (Sterling)

Hands-On Facts about Food and the Kitchen

Did you know . . .

- worker ants have two stomachs? The first stomach is used to process an ant's own food, while the second is used to store food that will be taken back to the colony for use by other ants.

- there are more than 400 kinds of cheese made throughout the world?

- you can tell how sharp the taste of a piece of Swiss cheese will be by the size of its holes? Large holes indicate that the cheese has been cured for a longer time, and the cheese will therefore have a stronger flavor. Small holes mean that the cheese is younger and will have a milder taste.

- mold is actually added to cheeses to improve their flavor? For example, moldy bread crumbs are added to Roquefort cheese. Without the addition of the mold, Roquefort wouldn't taste like Roquefort!

- brewer's yeast isn't just used by brewers to make beer? It can also be used to help prevent and cure illness, because it contains large amounts of B-complex vitamins.

- not all fats are bad for your heart? While saturated fats can increase the level of cholesterol in your blood, and thus increase your chances of suffering heart disease, polyunsaturated fats are thought to actually decrease blood cholesterol.

- flowers from squash and pumpkin plants aren't just colorful, but also good to eat? Check your family cookbooks, and you may find recipes for fried squash blossoms or pumpkin flower soup!

- the sugar you use to bake cookies or sweeten your breakfast cereal may have come from a root vegetable, the sugar beet?

- the tomatoes and peppers that are so good for you have a poisonous cousin? Tomatoes, peppers, and several other vegetables are members of the nightshade family of plants, which also includes the poisonous plant called deadly nightshade.

- some trees form lateral root systems that are much bigger than the tree they support? An oak tree that is 37 feet (11 m) high, for example, can have a root system that extends 60 feet (18 m) out from the base of the tree.

GLOSSARY

bacteria: one-cell, microscopic organisms. Some bacteria help us to digest food, others bring about decay, and still others, called "germs," cause disease.

biennial: a plant that requires two years to complete its growing cycle.

biogeography: the study and mapping of the living things on Earth.

botany: the scientific study of plants.

calcium: a chemical element found in milk and milk products that promotes the growth and maintenance of healthy bones and teeth.

calorie: a unit for measuring the amount of heat or energy that can be produced by a food.

carbohydrate: a compound, such as sugar or starch, that is composed of carbon, hydrogen, and oxygen.

cholesterol: a substance found in body cells and fluids that is thought to promote heart disease.

clabbering: the way milk separates into watery whey and more solid curds. The clabbering process is an essential step in the making of cheese.

crucifers: plants that are members of the mustard family, including broccoli, cauliflower, and radishes.

demography: the study of human populations.

fat: the oily or greasy substance in many meats, poultry, fish, nuts, and other foods. The body needs some fat to function well, but excess fat can cause serious health problems.

fermentation: the process by which sugar is broken down into carbon dioxide and alcohol.

lactose: the sugar that is naturally found in milk.

photosynthesis: the process by which plants convert sunlight into nutrients. Photosynthesis begins when chlorophyll in the leaves is activated by the sunlight.

protein: a substance that is found in all living plant and animal tissue. Protein contains nitrogen and is necessary to maintain life.

respiration: the process of taking in oxygen and then releasing carbon dioxide.

root, root vegetable: A root is the part of a plant that takes in water and minerals from the soil and keeps the plant in one place. Some roots, such as carrots and turnips, can be eaten as vegetables.

tuber: underground stems that are often mistaken for roots. The potato you eat for dinner is a tuber.

yeast: a substance consisting of tiny one-celled plants that use the energy that is a by-product of fermentation to support its own life-processes. Yeast is used in baking to make bread rise.

INDEX